THE ULTIMATE
SMOOTHIES RECIPES BOOK

A Life-Changing Way Including Recipes, Tips, and Tricks to Relieve Nausea, Vomiting and Other Symptoms.

CHRISTIANA WHITE

GAIN ACCESS TO MORE BOOKS

TABLE OF CONTENTS.

INTRODUCTION

Living with gastroparesis may be difficult since it causes the stomach to move improperly, causing symptoms including delayed gastric emptying, bloating, nausea, and pain in the abdomen. It might be difficult to maintain a diet that is suitable for people with gastroparesis and offers appropriate nutrients while reducing discomfort.

By offering smoothie recipes made especially for those with gastroparesis, this book seeks to provide a remedy. Smoothies are a useful and efficient solution to meet the special dietary requirements of gastroparesis patients.

We'll examine how smoothies may significantly enhance the health of those who have gastroparesis. We'll talk about the advantages of include smoothies in your diet, how they may provide important nutrients in an easily assailable form, and how they can help with gastroparesis symptoms.

People with gastroparesis may improve their digestion, reclaim control over their dietary intake, and feed their bodies in a tasty and practical manner by harnessing the power of smoothies. To help you manage your illness and enhance your quality of life, this book will lead you through a selection of expertly made smoothie recipes as well as provide lifestyle advice, ideas, and strategies.

Let's dive into the beautiful world of gastroparesis smoothies to start this path toward improved nutrition, symptom reduction, and general wellness.

CHAPTER 1

What Precisely Is Gastroparesis?

The medical disorder known as gastroparesis prevents the stomach's muscles from moving normally, which delays the passage of food into the small intestine. The term "gastroparesis" literally means "stomach paralysis," which accurately describes the disorder's decreased motility.

The muscles of the stomach contract regularly in a healthy digestive system to move food forward and combine it with digestive fluids.

This motion, referred to as gastric motility, aids in the breakdown of food and makes it easier for it to enter the small intestine for further digestion and absorption. Food stays in the stomach for a long time in gastroparesis because these muscular contractions are weak or non-existent.

Although the precise etiology of gastroparesis is not always known, it is often linked to injury to or malfunction of the vagus nerve, which regulates the muscles of the digestive tract. The onset of gastroparesis may be influenced by diseases including diabetes, autoimmune illnesses, neurological disorders, and certain drugs.

Understanding the Symptoms of Gastroparesis

Individuals might differ in their symptom intensity and frequency. The following are some typical signs and symptoms of gastroparesis:

- Vomiting and Nausea: Constant nausea is a typical sign of gastroparesis. Vomiting may accompany it and start many hours after eating or drinking.

- Abdominal bloating and pain are common symptoms of gastroparesis, as are feeling full fast and bloating after meals. These sensations may be exacerbated by the sense that food has been sitting in the stomach for a long time.

- Early Satiety: People with gastroparesis may feel satiated before finishing even a little quantity of food. It may be difficult to achieve dietary requirements and maintain a healthy weight because of this early satiety.

- Acid Reflux: Gastroparesis may cause stomach acid to reflux into the oesophagus, resulting in symptoms including heartburn, regurgitation, and a bitter aftertaste.

- Lack of Appetite: Due to the pain and early satiety experienced after eating, gastroparesis might reduce appetite. This may lead to decreased calorie consumption and possible weight reduction.

- Blood sugar fluctuations may occur in people with diabetes because gastroparesis interferes with the normal digestion and absorption of food. Diabetes control may become more difficult as a result.

- Nutritional shortages: Prolonged gastroparesis may interfere with the body's ability to absorb vital nutrients, possibly resulting in nutritional shortages. This may show up as weakness, exhaustion, and other malnutrition-related symptoms.

It is crucial to remember that not everyone who has gastroparesis will have the same combination of symptoms, and their severity might also differ. It is advised to speak with a healthcare provider for an accurate diagnosis and treatment if you think you may have gastroparesis or are exhibiting any of these symptoms.

Dietary changes, drugs to enhance stomach emptying, symptom management techniques, and treating any underlying reasons or contributing factors are all potential treatment options.

CHAPTER 2

The Fundamentals of Smoothies

As a fast and wholesome supper or snack, smoothies are becoming more and more well-liked. In a single glass, they provide a tasty and practical method to cram a range of nutrients.

Smoothies are a flexible and adaptable addition to your daily routine, whether you're wanting to increase your energy levels, improve your digestion, or just enjoy a refreshing treat.

You'll be able to adapt recipes to your own preferences, nutritional demands, and health objectives if you have a firm grasp of the foundations of smoothie-making.

Benefits of Smoothies for Patients with Gastroparesis

Smoothies may provide a variety of advantages for people with gastroparesis, including a number of advantages for symptom management and general nutrition enhancement. Incorporating smoothies into the diet of people with gastroparesis has a number of important advantages, including the following:

- Smoothies digest more readily than solid meals since they are liquid-based. Because components are broken down into tiny pieces during the blending process, the digestive system is less taxed and nutrients are more effectively absorbed.

- Rich in nutrients: Gastroparesis may cause poor nutritional absorption and malnutrition. Smoothies may include nutrient-dense components such fruits, vegetables, proteins, good fats, and liquids. They provide you a quick and easy method to get the antioxidants, vitamins, and minerals you need for good health.

- Smoothies may be made to fit certain dietary requirements and tastes. They are flexible and customizable. Specific food intolerances, allergies, or dietary restrictions may be accommodated by making adjustments to these dishes. Because of their adaptability, ingredients may be chosen from a broad variety to fit dietary needs and preferences.

- Increased Fiber Intake: Because high-fiber foods are harder to digest when one has gastroparesis, one may consume more fiber. Smoothies may be made more filling by adding sources of soluble fiber, such as oats, flaxseeds, or chia seeds, which are easier to handle and may aid in a healthy digestive system.

- Water intake: Those who have gastroparesis must keep themselves well hydrated. Smoothies may be created with hydrating components like coconut water, herbal teas, or low-acid fruit juices, which serve to avoid dehydration and enhance general wellbeing.

Smoothies may assist in managing the symptoms of gastroparesis, including bloating, nausea, and early satiety.

Instead of the agony and anxiety that typical solid meals might bring, they can provide a soft and calming solution for sustenance.

Blood Sugar Control: Smoothies that include a well-balanced combination of carbs, proteins, and fats may be made for those with diabetes and gastroparesis.

As carbohydrates are released into the circulation gradually, this may aid in controlling blood sugar levels.

How to Choose the Best Ingredients

Making smoothies for those with gastroparesis requires careful consideration of the components.

Fruits that are easy to digest and less prone to cause pain are the best choice. Bananas, ripe avocados, cooked apples or pears, and melons (like cantaloupe and honeydew) are among examples. The smoothie gets its natural sweetness from these fruits, which are often well-tolerated.

Veggies that have been cooked or steam-cooked are easier for people with gastroparesis to digest than raw veggies. Use veggies like pumpkin, zucchini, spinach, or carrots that have been boiled or steamed. While still offering important nutrients, these softer veggies are kinder on the stomach.

Select readily digested forms of protein for your diet. Greek yogurt, silken tofu, nut butters (such almond or cashew), and protein powders created expressly for sensitive stomachs are possible alternatives. Protein maintains the health of muscles while also promoting satiety.

Enhance healthy fats to your diet to enhance richness and give nutrients that are necessary. An avocado, a little quantity of nuts or seeds, coconut milk, flaxseed oil, or coconut oil are all suitable options.

The fat-soluble vitamins are more easily absorbed thanks to these lipids.

Almond milk, coconut water, herbal teas, or low-acid fruit juices are some examples of beverages that are easy on the stomach.

Without aggravating symptoms, these beverages may hydrate you and help you reach the right consistency.

Take into account soluble forms of fiber, such as chia seeds or ground flaxseeds, for those who can handle them. While promoting proper digestion and offering additional nutritional advantages, they won't add much to body mass.

Consider enhancing the taste by adding natural ingredients like ginger, mint, cinnamon, or vanilla essence. Without irritating the digestive system, they may give the smoothie a pleasing flavor.

Individual tolerances for certain substances might differ, it's crucial to remember that. It is advised to maintain a food journal and monitor your symptoms to find any triggers or intolerances.

You may get individualized advice on ingredient selection based on your unique requirements and sensitivities by speaking with a healthcare practitioner or registered dietician.

How to Prepare Smoothies: Equipment and Methods

By using the proper tools and following certain procedures, making smoothies may be done more quickly and easily. For making smoothies, the following tools and procedures are necessary:

Equipment:

Blender: Invest in a strong blender of the highest caliber that can handle mixing a range of components, including frozen fruits and vegetables. For a smooth, reliable output, look for a blender with a powerful engine and cutting-edge blades.

To achieve precise measurements of the components, use measuring spoons, cups, or a kitchen scale. Across several batches of smoothies, this helps maintain uniformity in flavor and texture.

For chopping and preparing fresh fruits and vegetables, a good cutting board and a sharp knife are necessary. In order to prepare components for mixing, you may quickly chop, slice, and dice.

Optional: Use a fine-mesh strainer or nut milk bag to filter the smoothie after mixing if you like a smoother texture or want to get rid of any fibrous particles.

Techniques:

Layering: Putting the ingredients in the blender in layers may help them mix better and save the motor from overworking. Starting at the bottom, layer liquid or softer components, then top with frozen or harder ones.

Liquid-to-Ingredient Ratio: Pour the liquid (such as coconut water or almond milk) into the blender first, then add the remaining ingredients. With a smoother consistency, this makes mixing easier.

The smoothie's desired thickness will determine how much liquid to add.

Blending with a gradual rise in speed: Start the blender at a low speed and work your way up to one that is faster. By preventing air pockets from developing, this aids in the uniform breakdown of the contents.

Stop the blender every so often, and use a spatula to scrape the sides clean. By doing this, you can make sure that every ingredient is mixed in equally and that no pieces remain unmixed.

Frozen or Iced Ingredients Should Be Added Last: Once all other ingredients have been well combined, add any ice cubes or frozen fruits and vegetables. By doing this, a smooth and creamy texture is ensured and excessive straining is avoided.

Changing Consistency: If the smoothie is too thick, gradually add more liquid while blending again until you get the desired consistency. To make it thicker if it's too thin, add additional ice cubes or frozen ingredients.

To prevent any mishaps, always use the blender according to the manufacturer's instructions and handle the tools carefully. You can make well-blended, tasty smoothies that are customized to your tastes and dietary requirements with the correct tools and methods.

CHAPTER 3

Smoothie Recipes for Breakfast

Smoothie with Bananas and Peanut Butter

One Servings

Ingredients

- 1 cup (240 mL) milk (or other non-dairy milk of choice)
- 1/4 cup creamy peanut butter (60 g)
- 1 large peeled and sliced banana
- 1 tablespoon vanilla extract
- A dash of salt
- As needed, ice cubes

Method

- Combine the milk, peanut butter, banana, vanilla extract, and salt in a blender. Blend until the mixture is smooth and creamy.
- Blend in the ice cubes until the smoothie achieves the desired consistency.
- Serve the smoothie in a big glass or dish.

Nutritional Information

- 520 calories
- 19 g protein
- Fat: 31 g
- 49 g carbohydrate
- 5 g fiber
- 30 g sugar

Smoothie with Fresh Berries

One Servings

Ingredients

- 1 cup (150 g) fresh or frozen mixed berries
- 1/2 cup (120 mL) vanilla low-fat yogurt
- 1/4 cup (60 mL) milk (or other nondairy milk of choice)
- 1 teaspoon of honey
- As needed, ice cubes

Method

- Blend the berries, yogurt, milk, and honey in a blender. Blend until the mixture is smooth and foamy.
- Blend in the ice cubes until the smoothie achieves the desired consistency.

- Serve the smoothie in a big glass or dish.

Nutritional Information

- 260 calories
- 9 g protein
- Fat: 3 g
- 53 g carbohydrate
- 5 g fiber
- 46 g sugar

Smoothie with Apples and Cinnamon

One Servings

Ingredients

- 1 cup apple juice (240 mL)
- 1/4 cup (20 g) low-fiber or refined cereal (for example, corn flakes or rice crispies)
- 1 tablespoon cinnamon
- A dash of nutmeg
- As needed, ice cubes

Method

- Combine the apple juice, cereal, cinnamon, and nutmeg in a blender. Blend until smooth and thoroughly incorporated.

- Blend in the ice cubes until the smoothie achieves the desired consistency.
- Serve the smoothie in a big glass or dish.

Nutritional Information

- 180 calories
- 2 g protein
- Fat: 0 g
- 44 g carbohydrate
- 1 g fiber
- 32 g sugar

Smoothie Made With Vanilla Latte

One Servings

Ingredients

- 1 cup (240 mL) chilled brewed decaffeinated coffee
- 1/4 cup (60 mL) milk (or other nondairy milk of choice)
- 2 teaspoons vanilla pudding mix
- 1 tablespoon vanilla extract
- As needed, ice cubes

Method

- Blend the coffee, milk, pudding mix, and vanilla extract in a blender. Blend until the mixture is smooth and creamy.
- Blend in the ice cubes until the smoothie achieves the desired consistency.
- Serve the smoothie in a big glass or dish.

Nutritional Information

- 140 calories
- 4 g protein
- Fat: 2 g
- 26 g carbohydrate
- Fiber content: 0 g
- 18 g sugar

Smoothie with Tropical Fruits

One Servings

Ingredients

- 1/2 cup pineapple juice (120 mL)
- 1/4 cup orange juice (60 mL)
- 1/4 cup (60 g) chopped canned or fresh mango
- 1/4 cup (40 g) chopped canned or fresh papaya

- As needed, ice cubes

Method

- Combine the pineapple juice, orange juice, mango, and papaya in a blender. Blend until the mixture is smooth and fruity.
- Blend in the ice cubes until the smoothie achieves the desired consistency.
- Serve the smoothie in a big glass or dish.

Nutritional Information

- 160 calories
- 1 g protein
- Fat: 0 g
- 40 g carbohydrates
- 2 g fiber
- 34 g sugar

Smoothie with Carrot Cake

One Servings

Ingredients

- 1/2 cup carrot juice (120 mL)
- 1 tablespoon (60 g) low-fat cream cheese
- 2 teaspoons brown sugar
- 1 tablespoon cinnamon
- A dash of nutmeg
- As needed, ice cubes

Method

- Combine the carrot juice, cream cheese, brown sugar, cinnamon, and nutmeg in a blender. Blend until the mixture is smooth and creamy.
- Blend in the ice cubes until the smoothie achieves the desired consistency.
- Serve the smoothie in a big glass or dish.

Nutritional Information

- 240 calories
- 6 g protein
- Fat: 9 g
- 36 g carbohydrate

- 1 g fiber
- 31 g sugar

Smoothie with Oatmeal and Raisins

One Servings

Ingredients

- 1/2 cup (120 mL) milk (or other non-dairy milk of choice)
- 1/4 cup quick-cooking oats (20 g)
- 2 teaspoons raisins
- 1 teaspoon maple syrup
- 1 tablespoon vanilla extract
- A dash of salt
- As needed, ice cubes

Method

- Blend together the milk, oats, raisins, maple syrup, vanilla extract, and salt in a blender. Blend until smooth and thoroughly incorporated.
- Blend in the ice cubes until the smoothie achieves the desired consistency.
- Serve the smoothie in a big glass or dish.

Nutritional Information

- 260 calories
- 7 g protein
- Fat: 4 g
- 51 g carbohydrate
- 3 g fiber
- 30 g sugar

Smoothie with Kiwi and Lime

One Servings

Ingredients

- 1/2 cup limeade (120 mL)
- 1/4 cup plain yogurt (60 g)
- 2 peeled and sliced kiwis
- As needed, ice cubes

Method

- Blend the limeade, yogurt, and kiwis in a blender. Blend until the mixture is smooth and tangy.
- Blend in the ice cubes until the smoothie achieves the desired consistency.
- Serve the smoothie in a big glass or dish.

Nutritional Information

- 180 calories
- 5 g protein
- Fat: 2 g
- 39 g carbohydrate
- 4 g fiber
- 31 g sugar

Smoothie with Almond Joy

One Servings

Ingredients

- 1/2 cup (120 mL) chocolate milk (or your favorite non-dairy chocolate milk)
- 1/4 cup vanilla yogurt (60 g)
- 2 teaspoons shredded coconut
- 1 teaspoon almond butter
- As needed, ice cubes

Method

- Blend together the chocolate milk, yogurt, coconut, and almond butter in a blender. Blend until the mixture is smooth and chocolate.

- Blend in the ice cubes until the smoothie achieves the desired consistency.
- Serve the smoothie in a big glass or dish.

Nutritional Information

• 320 calories

• 11 g protein

• Fat: 18 g

• 34 g carbohydrate

• 4 g fiber

• 28 g sugar

Smoothie with Cranberries and Oranges

One Servings

Ingredients

- 1/2 cup cranberry juice (120 mL)
- 1/4 cup orange juice (60 mL)
- 1/4 cup plain yogurt (60 g)
- 1 teaspoon of honey
- As needed, ice cubes

Method

- Blend together the cranberry juice, orange juice, yogurt, and honey in a blender. Blend until the mixture is smooth and refreshing.
- Blend in the ice cubes until the smoothie achieves the desired consistency.
- Serve the smoothie in a big glass or dish.

Nutritional Information

- 180 calories
- 4 g protein
- Fat: 1 g
- 42 g carbohydrate
- 1 g fiber
- 39 g sugar

CHAPTER 4

Lunch Smoothies Recipes

Smoothie with Carrots and Ginger

One Servings

Ingredients

- 1 cup carrot juice (240 mL)
- 1/4 cup plain yogurt (60 g)
- 1 teaspoon of honey
- 1 tablespoon ginger
- As needed, ice cubes

Method

- Blend the carrot juice, yogurt, honey, and ginger in a blender. Blend until the mixture is smooth and spicy.
- Blend in the ice cubes until the smoothie achieves the desired consistency.
- Serve the smoothie in a big glass or dish.

Nutritional Information

- 180 calories
- 5 g protein
- Fat: 1 g
- 40 g carbohydrates
- 1 g fiber
- 36 g sugar

Smoothie with Creamy Tomatoes

One Servings

Ingredients

- 1 cup tomato juice (240 mL)
- 1 tablespoon (60 g) low-fat cream cheese
- 1 tablespoon fresh basil
- Season with salt and pepper to taste
- As needed, ice cubes

Method

- Combine the tomato juice, cream cheese, basil, salt, and pepper in a blender. Blend until the mixture is smooth and creamy.

- Blend in the ice cubes until the smoothie achieves the desired consistency.
- Serve the smoothie in a big glass or dish.

Nutritional Information

- 200 calories
- 8 g protein
- Fat: 10 g
- 20 g carbohydrates
- 2 g fiber
- 14 g sugar

Smoothie with Spinach and Avocado

One Servings

Ingredients

- 1/2 cup vegetable juice (120 mL)
- 1/4 cup (60 g) peeled and diced avocado
- 1 tablespoon (15 g) baby spinach
- 1 teaspoon lemon juice
- As needed, ice cubes

Method

- Blend the vegetable juice, avocado, spinach, and lemon juice in a blender. Blend until the mixture is smooth and green.
- Blend in the ice cubes until the smoothie achieves the desired consistency.
- Serve the smoothie in a big glass or dish.

Nutritional Information

- 160 calories
- 3 g protein
- Fat: 12 g
- 14 g carbohydrate
- 6 g fiber
- 8 g sugar

Smoothie with Peaches and Mangoes

One Servings

Ingredients

- 1/2 cup peach juice (120 mL)
- 1/4 cup (60 g) chopped canned or fresh mango
- 1/4 cup plain yogurt (60 g)
- 1 teaspoon of honey

- As needed, ice cubes

Method

- Blend the peach juice, mango, yogurt, and honey in a blender. Blend until the mixture is smooth and fruity.
- Blend in the ice cubes until the smoothie achieves the desired consistency.
- Serve the smoothie in a big glass or dish.

Nutritional Information

- 200 calories
- 5 g protein
- Fat: 1 g
- 46 g carbohydrate
- 2 g fiber
- 42 g sugar

Smoothie with Chocolate and Banana

One Servings

Ingredients

- 1/2 cup (120 mL) chocolate milk (or your favorite non-dairy chocolate milk)
- 1/4 cup (60 g) peeled and sliced banana

- 1/4 cup vanilla yogurt (60 g)
- As needed, ice cubes

Method

- Combine the chocolate milk, banana, and yogurt in a blender. Blend until the mixture is smooth and chocolate.
- Blend in the ice cubes until the smoothie achieves the desired consistency.
- Serve the smoothie in a big glass or dish.

Nutritional Information

- 240 calories
- 9 g protein
- Fat: 4 g
- 44 g carbohydrate
- 3 g fiber
- 36 g sugar

Smoothie with Cucumber and Mint

One Servings

Ingredients

- 1/2 cup water (120 mL)
- 1/4 cup (60 g) peeled and sliced cucumber
- A quarter cup (15 g) fresh mint leaves
- 1 teaspoon lime juice
- 1 tablespoon sugar
- As needed, ice cubes

Method

- Blend together the water, cucumber, mint, lime juice, and sugar in a blender. Blend until the mixture is smooth and refreshing.
- Blend in the ice cubes until the smoothie achieves the desired consistency.
- Serve the smoothie in a big glass or dish.

Nutritional Information

- 40 calories
- 1 g protein
- Fat: 0 g
- 10 g carbohydrates

- 1 g fiber
- 7 g sugar

Smoothie with Sweet Potato Pie

One Servings

Ingredients

- 1/2 cup (120 mL) milk (or other non-dairy milk of choice)
- 1/4 cup (60 g) mashed cooked sweet potato
- 1/4 cup vanilla yogurt (60 g)
- 1 teaspoon brown sugar
- 1 tablespoon cinnamon
- A dash of nutmeg
- As needed, ice cubes

Method

- Blend together the milk, sweet potato, yogurt, brown sugar, cinnamon, and nutmeg in a blender. Blend until the mixture is smooth and creamy.
- Blend in the ice cubes until the smoothie achieves the desired consistency.
- Serve the smoothie in a big glass or dish.

Nutritional Information

- 220 calories
- 7 g protein
- Fat: 3 g
- 44 g carbohydrate
- 3 g fiber
- 34 g sugar

Smoothie with Pineapple and Coconut

One Servings

Ingredients

- 1/2 cup pineapple juice (120 mL)
- 1/4 cup coconut milk (60 mL)
- 1/4 cup (60 g) chopped canned or fresh pineapple
- 1 teaspoon shredded coconut
- As needed, ice cubes

Method

- Blend together the pineapple juice, coconut milk, pineapple, and shredded coconut in a blender. Blend till smooth and tropical-flavoured.

- Blend in the ice cubes until the smoothie achieves the desired consistency.
- Serve the smoothie in a big glass or dish.

Nutritional Information

- 240 calories
- 2 g protein
- Fat: 14 g
- 30 g carbohydrates
- 3 g fiber
- 24 g sugar

Smoothie with Peanut Butter and Jelly

One Servings

Ingredients

- 1/2 cup (120 mL) milk (or other non-dairy milk of choice)
- 1/4 cup creamy peanut butter (60 g)
- 1/4 cup grape jelly (60 g)
- As needed, ice cubes

Method

- Combine the milk, peanut butter, and jelly in a blender. Blend until smooth and creamy.
- Blend in the ice cubes until the smoothie achieves the desired consistency.
- Serve the smoothie in a big glass or dish.

Nutritional Information

- 480 calories
- 16 g protein
- Fat: 24 g
- 56 g carbohydrate
- 3 g fiber
- 40 g sugar

Smoothie with Apple Pie

One Servings

Ingredients

- 1/2 cup apple juice (120 mL)
- 1/4 cup applesauce (60 g)
- 1/4 cup vanilla yogurt (60 g)
- 1 teaspoon brown sugar

- 1 tablespoon cinnamon
- A dash of nutmeg
- As needed, ice cubes

Method

- Blend together the apple juice, applesauce, yogurt, brown sugar, cinnamon, and nutmeg in a blender. Blend until the mixture is smooth and delicious.
- Blend in the ice cubes until the smoothie achieves the desired consistency.
- Serve the smoothie in a big glass or dish.

Nutritional Information

- 220 calories
- 5 g protein
- Fat: 1 g
- 50 g carbohydrates
- 2 g fiber
- 44 g sugar

CHAPTER 5

Recipes for Snack Smoothies

Smoothie with Strawberries and Yogurt

One Servings

Ingredients

- 1/2 cup strawberry juice (120 mL)
- 1 tablespoon (60 g) strawberry yogurt
- 1/4 cup (37 g) diced canned or fresh strawberries
- As needed, ice cubes

Method

- Blend together the strawberry juice, yogurt, and strawberries in a blender. Blend until the mixture is smooth and pink.
- Blend in the ice cubes until the smoothie reaches the desired consistency.
- Serve the smoothie in a large glass or bowl.

Nutritional Information

- 160 calories
- 5 g protein
- Fat: 2 g

- 34 g carbohydrate
- 2 g fiber
- 30 g sugar

Smoothie with Pumpkin Pie

One Servings

Ingredients

- 1/2 cup (120 mL) milk (or other non-dairy milk of choice)
- 1/4 cup canned pumpkin puree (60 g)
- 1/4 cup vanilla yogurt (60 g)
- 1 teaspoon brown sugar
- 1 tablespoon pumpkin pie spice
- As needed, ice cubes

Method

- Blend together the milk, pumpkin, yogurt, brown sugar, and pumpkin pie spice in a blender. Blend until the mixture is smooth and orange.
- Blend in the ice cubes until the smoothie reaches the desired consistency.
- Serve the smoothie in a large glass or bowl.

Nutritional Information

- 200 calories
- 7 g protein
- Fat: 3 g
- 38 g carbohydrate
- 3 g fiber
- 32 g sugar

Smoothie with Blueberries and Muffins

One Servings

Ingredients

- 1/2 cup blueberry juice (120 mL)
- 1/4 cup (20 g) low-fiber or refined cereal (for example, corn flakes or rice crispies)
- 1/4 cup vanilla yogurt (60 g)
- 1 teaspoon of honey
- As needed, ice cubes

Method

- Blend together the blueberry juice, cereal, yogurt, and honey in a blender. Blend until the mixture is smooth and purple.

- Blend in the ice cubes until the smoothie reaches the desired consistency.
- Serve the smoothie in a large glass or bowl.

Nutritional Information

- 220 calories
- 6 g protein
- Fat: 1 g
- 49 g carbohydrate
- 1 g fiber
- 40 g sugar

Smoothie with Lemon Cheesecake

One Servings

Ingredients

- 1/2 cup lemonade (120 mL)
- 1 tablespoon (60 g) low-fat cream cheese
- 1/4 cup vanilla yogurt (60 g)
- 1 tablespoon crushed graham crackers
- As needed, ice cubes

Method

- Combine the lemonade, cream cheese, yogurt, and graham cracker crumbs in a blender. Blend until the mixture is smooth and yellow.
- Blend in the ice cubes until the smoothie reaches the desired consistency.
- Serve the smoothie in a large glass or bowl.

Nutritional Information

- 240 calories

- 9 g protein

- Fat: 9 g

- 33 g carbohydrate

- 1 g fiber

- 25 g sugar

Smoothie with Cherries and Almonds

One Servings

Ingredients

- 1/2 cup cherry juice (120 mL)

- 1/4 cup plain yogurt (60 g)
- 1/4 cup (37 g) pitted and diced canned or fresh cherries
- 1 teaspoon almond butter
- As needed, ice cubes

Method

- Blend together the cherry juice, yogurt, cherries, and almond butter in a blender. Blend until the mixture is smooth and red.
- Blend in the ice cubes until the smoothie reaches the desired consistency.
- Serve the smoothie in a large glass or bowl.

Nutritional Information

- 240 calories
- 9 g protein
- Fat: 11 g
- 30 g carbohydrates
- 3 g fiber
- 24 g sugar

Smoothie Made From Banana Bread

One Servings

Ingredients

- 1/2 cup (120 mL) milk (or other nondairy milk of choice)
- 1/4 cup (60 g) peeled and sliced banana
- 1/4 cup (20 g) low-fiber or refined cereal (for example, corn flakes or rice crispies)
- 1 teaspoon brown sugar
- 1 tablespoon cinnamon
- A dash of nutmeg
- As needed, ice cubes

Method

- Blend together the milk, banana, cereal, brown sugar, cinnamon, and nutmeg in a blender. Blend until the mixture is smooth and creamy.
- Blend in the ice cubes until the smoothie reaches the desired consistency.
- Serve the smoothie in a large glass or bowl.

Nutritional Information

- 220 calories
- 6 g protein
- Fat: 2 g
- 48 g carbohydrate
- 2 g fiber
- 34 g sugar

Smoothie with Raspberries and Lemonade

One Servings

Ingredients

- 1/2 cup lemonade (120 mL)
- 1/4 cup (37 g) fresh or canned raspberries
- 1/4 cup plain yogurt (60 g)
- 1 teaspoon of honey
- As needed, ice cubes

Method

- Blend the lemonade, raspberries, yogurt, and honey in a blender. Blend until the mixture is smooth and pink.
- Blend in the ice cubes until the smoothie achieves the desired consistency.

- Serve the smoothie in a big glass or dish.

Nutritional Information

- 180 calories
- 5 g protein
- Fat: 1 g
- 40 g carbohydrates
- 3 g fiber
- Sugar: 35 g

Pina Colada Smoothie

One Servings

Ingredients

- 1/2 cup pineapple juice (120 mL)
- 1/4 cup coconut milk (60 mL)
- 1/4 cup (60 g) chopped canned or fresh pineapple
- 1 teaspoon shredded coconut
- As needed, ice cubes

Method

- Blend together the pineapple juice, coconut milk, pineapple, and shredded coconut in a blender. Blend till smooth and tropical-flavored.

- Blend in the ice cubes until the smoothie achieves the desired consistency.
- Serve the smoothie in a big glass or dish.

Nutritional Information

- 240 calories
- 2 g protein
- Fat: 14 g
- 30 g carbohydrates
- 3 g fiber
- 24 g sugar

Smoothie with Chocolate Chip Cookie

One Servings

Ingredients

- 1/2 cup (120 mL) milk (or other non-dairy milk of choice)
- 1/4 cup vanilla yogurt (60 g)
- 1/4 cup (20 g) low-fiber or refined cereal (for example, corn flakes or rice crispies)
- 1 teaspoon tiny chocolate chips
- 1 tablespoon vanilla extract
- As needed, ice cubes

Method

- Blend together the milk, yogurt, cereal, chocolate chips, and vanilla extract in a blender. Blend until the mixture is smooth and chocolate.
- Blend in the ice cubes until the smoothie achieves the desired consistency.
- Serve the smoothie in a big glass or dish.

Nutritional Information

- 260 calories
- 7 g protein
- Fat: 8 g
- 42 g carbohydrate
- 2 g fiber
- 30 g sugar

Smoothie with Orange Creamsicle

One Servings

Ingredients

- 1/2 cup orange juice (120 mL)
- 1/4 cup vanilla yogurt (60 g)
- 1/4 cup vanilla pudding mix (60 g)

- As needed, ice cubes

Method

- Combine the orange juice, yogurt, and pudding mix in a blender. Blend until the mixture is smooth and creamy.
- Blend in the ice cubes until the smoothie achieves the desired consistency.
- Serve the smoothie in a big glass or dish.

Nutritional Information

- 200 calories
- 6 g protein
- Fat: 3 g
- 38 g carbohydrate
- Fiber content: 0 g
- 30 g sugar

CHAPTER 6

Smoothies for Dinner

Smoothie with Chicken Noodles

One Servings

Ingredients

- 1 cup chicken broth (240 mL)
- 1/4 cup (30 g) shredded cooked chicken
- 1/4 cup (20 g) chopped cooked noodles
- 1 tablespoon creamed chicken soup
- Season with salt and pepper to taste
- As needed, ice cubes

Method

- Blend the chicken broth, chicken, noodles, and cream of chicken soup, salt, and pepper in a blender. Blend until the mixture is smooth and flavourful.
- Blend in the ice cubes until the smoothie achieves the desired consistency.
- Serve the smoothie in a big glass or dish.

Nutritional Information

- 200 calories
- 15 g protein
- Fat: 8 g
- 18 g carbohydrate
- 1 g fiber
- 2 g sugar

Smoothie with Roasted Vegetables

One Servings

Ingredients

- 1/2 cup veggie broth (120 mL)
- 1/4 cup (60 g) roasted veggies (carrots, zucchini, squash)
- 1/4 cup plain yogurt (60 g)
- 1 teaspoon tomato paste
- Season with salt and pepper to taste
- As needed, ice cubes

Method

- Blend together the vegetable broth, roasted veggies, yogurt, tomato paste, salt, and pepper in a blender. Blend until the mixture is smooth and hearty.

- Blend in the ice cubes until the smoothie achieves the desired consistency.
- Serve the smoothie in a big glass or dish.

Nutritional Information

- 120 calories
- 5 g protein
- Fat: 2 g
- 20 g carbohydrates
- 3 g fiber
- 12 g sugar

Smoothie with Mushroom Soup

One Servings

Ingredients

- 1 cup mushroom broth (240 mL)
- 1/4 cup (40 g) sliced cooked mushrooms
- 1 tablespoon (60 g) low-fat cream cheese
- 1 teaspoon sour cream
- Season with salt and pepper to taste
- As needed, ice cubes

Method

- Blend together the mushroom broth, mushrooms, cream cheese, sour cream, salt, and pepper in a blender. Blend until the mixture is smooth and creamy.
- Blend in the ice cubes until the smoothie achieves the desired consistency.
- Serve the smoothie in a big glass or dish.

Nutritional Information

- 180 calories
- 8 g protein
- Fat: 12 g
- 10 g carbohydrates
- 1 g fiber
- 6 g sugar

Smoothie with Beef Stew

One Servings

Ingredients

- 1 cup beef broth (240 mL)
- 1/4 cup (40 g) diced cooked beef
- 1/4 cup (60 g) mashed cooked potatoes
- 1 tablespoon sauce
- Season with salt and pepper to taste
- As needed, ice cubes

Method

- Blend the beef broth, beef, potatoes, gravy, salt, and pepper in a blender. Blend until the mixture is smooth and meaty.
- Blend in the ice cubes until the smoothie achieves the desired consistency.
- Serve the smoothie in a big glass or dish.

Nutritional Information

- 220 calories
- 15 g protein
- Fat: 10 g
- 18 g carbohydrate
- 2 g fiber

- 2 g sugar

Smoothie with Coconut and Curry

One Servings

Ingredients

- 1/2 cup coconut milk (120 mL)
- 1/4 cup (60 g) shredded cooked chicken
- 1/4 cup plain yogurt (60 g)
- 1 teaspoon curry paste
- Season with salt and pepper to taste
- As needed, ice cubes

Method

- Blend together the coconut milk, chicken, yogurt, curry paste, salt, and pepper in a blender. Blend until the mixture is smooth and spicy.
- Blend in the ice cubes until the smoothie achieves the desired consistency.
- Serve the smoothie in a big glass or dish.

Nutritional Information

- 300 calories
- 17 g protein
- Fat: 20 g
- 14 g carbohydrate
- 1 g fiber
- 10 g sugar

Smoothie with Butternut Squash

One Servings

Ingredients

- 1/2 cup veggie broth (120 mL)
- 1/4 cup (60 g) mashed cooked butternut squash
- 1/4 cup plain yogurt (60 g)
- 1 tablespoon of maple syrup
- 1 tablespoon cinnamon
- A dash of nutmeg
- As needed, ice cubes

Method

- In a blender, combine the vegetable broth, butternut squash, yogurt, maple syrup, cinnamon, and nutmeg. Blend until smooth and sweet.
- Blend in the ice cubes until the smoothie achieves the desired consistency.
- Serve the smoothie in a big glass or dish.

Nutritional Information

- Calories: 160
- 5 g protein
- Fat: 2 g
- Carbohydrates: 32 g
- 3 g fiber
- Sugar: 24 g

Minestrone Smoothie

One Servings

Ingredients

- 1 cup (240 ml) of vegetable broth
- 1/4 cup (60 g) of cooked mixed vegetables, such as carrots, celery, or green beans

- 1/4 cup (60 g) of cooked pasta, chopped
- 1 teaspoon tomato paste
- Season with salt and pepper to taste
- As needed, ice cubes

Method

- In a blender, combine the vegetable broth, mixed vegetables, pasta, tomato paste, salt, and pepper. Blend until the mixture is smooth and hearty.
- Blend in the ice cubes until the smoothie achieves the desired consistency.
- Serve the smoothie in a big glass or dish.

Nutritional Information

- Calories: 140
- 5 g protein
- Fat: 1 g
- Carbohydrates: 28 g
- Fiber: 4 g
- 10 g sugar

Chicken and Rice Smoothie

One Servings

Ingredients

- 1 cup chicken broth (240 mL)
- 1/4 cup (40 g) of cooked chicken, shredded
- 1/4 cup (50 g) of cooked rice, mashed
- 1 tablespoon creamed chicken soup
- Season with salt and pepper to taste
- As needed, ice cubes

Method

- In a blender, combine the chicken broth, chicken, rice, cream of chicken soup, salt, and pepper. Blend until the mixture is smooth and flavorful.
- Blend in the ice cubes until the smoothie achieves the desired consistency.
- Serve the smoothie in a big glass or dish.

Nutritional Information

- 200 calories
- 15 g protein
- Fat: 6 g
- Carbohydrates: 22 g

- 1 g fiber
- 2 g sugar

Lentil Soup Smoothie

One Servings

Ingredients

- 1 cup (240 ml) of vegetable broth
- 1/4 cup (50 g) of cooked lentils, mashed
- 1/4 cup plain yogurt (60 g)
- 1 teaspoon tomato paste
- Season with salt and pepper to taste
- As needed, ice cubes

Method

- In a blender, combine the vegetable broth, lentils, yogurt, tomato paste, salt, and pepper. Blend until smooth and full.
- Blend in the ice cubes until the smoothie achieves the desired consistency.
- Serve the smoothie in a big glass or dish.

Nutritional Information

- Calories: 180
- Protein: 12 g
- Fat: 2 g
- Carbohydrates: 30 g
- Fiber: 8 g
- 12 g sugar

Tomato Basil Smoothie

One Servings

Ingredients

- 1 cup (240 ml) of tomato juice
- 1/4 cup plain yogurt (60 g)
- 1 tablespoon of basil
- Season with salt and pepper to taste
- As needed, ice cubes

Method

- In a blender, combine the tomato juice, yogurt, basil, salt, and pepper. Blend until smooth and refreshing.
- Blend in the ice cubes until the smoothie achieves the desired consistency.

- Serve the smoothie in a big glass or dish.

Nutritional Information

- Calories: 100
- 5 g protein
- Fat: 1 g
- 18 g carbohydrate
- 2 g fiber

CHAPTER 7

Smoothies for Dessert

Smoothie with Chocolate and Mint

One Servings

Ingredients

- 1/2 cup (120 mL) chocolate milk (or your favorite non-dairy chocolate milk)
- 1/4 cup vanilla yogurt (60 g)
- 1/4 cup vanilla pudding mix (60 g)
- 1 tablespoon peppermint extract
- As needed, ice cubes

Method

- Blend together the chocolate milk, yogurt, pudding mix, and peppermint essence in a blender. Blend till the mixture is smooth and minty.
- Blend in the ice cubes until the smoothie achieves the desired consistency.
- Serve the smoothie in a big glass or dish.

Nutritional Information

- 240 calories
- 8 g protein
- Fat: 5 g
- 42 g carbohydrate
- 1 g fiber
- 34 g sugar

Smoothie with Raspberry Sorbet

One Servings

Ingredients

- 1/2 cup raspberry juice (120 mL)
- 1/4 cup raspberry sorbet (60 g)
- 1/4 cup plain yogurt (60 g)
- 1 teaspoon of honey
- As needed, ice cubes

Method

- Blend together the raspberry juice, sorbet, yogurt, and honey in a blender. Blend until the mixture is smooth and refreshing.

- Blend in the ice cubes until the smoothie achieves the desired consistency.
- Serve the smoothie in a big glass or dish.

Nutritional Information

- 220 calories
- 4 g protein
- Fat: 1 g
- 50 g carbohydrates
- 2 g fiber
- 44 g sugar

Smoothie with Key Lime Pie

One Servings

Ingredients

- 1/2 cup limeade (120 mL)
- 1 tablespoon (60 g) low-fat cream cheese
- 1/4 cup vanilla yogurt (60 g)
- 1 tablespoon crushed graham crackers
- As needed, ice cubes

Method

- Blend the limeade, cream cheese, yogurt, and graham cracker crumbs in a blender. Blend until the mixture is smooth and tangy.
- Blend in the ice cubes until the smoothie achieves the desired consistency.
- Serve the smoothie in a big glass or dish.

Nutritional Information

- 240 calories
- 9 g protein
- Fat: 9 g
- 33 g carbohydrate
- 1 g fiber
- 25 g sugar

Smoothie with Caramel Apples

One Servings

Ingredients

- 1/2 cup apple juice (120 mL)
- 1/4 cup applesauce (60 g)
- 1/4 cup vanilla yogurt (60 g)

- 1 teaspoon caramel sauce
- 1 tablespoon cinnamon
- As needed, ice cubes

Method

- Blend together the apple juice, applesauce, yogurt, caramel sauce, and cinnamon in a blender. Blend until the mixture is smooth and sweet.
- Blend in the ice cubes until the smoothie achieves the desired consistency.
- Serve the smoothie in a big glass or dish.

Nutritional Information

- 220 calories
- 5 g protein
- Fat: 3 g
- 46 g carbohydrate
- 2 g fiber
- 40 g sugar

Smoothie with Brownie Batter

One Servings

Ingredients

- 1/2 cup (120 mL) chocolate milk (or your favorite non-dairy chocolate milk)
- 1 tablespoon (60 g) chocolate yogurt
- 1/4 cup chocolate pudding mix (60 g)
- 1 teaspoon tiny chocolate chips
- As needed, ice cubes

Method

- Blend together the chocolate milk, yogurt, pudding mix, and chocolate chips in a blender. Blend until the mixture is smooth and chocolatey.
- Blend in the ice cubes until the smoothie achieves the desired consistency.
- Serve the smoothie in a big glass or dish.

Nutritional Information

- 320 calories
- 9 g protein
- Fat: 11 g
- 52 g carbohydrate

- 2 g fiber
- 44 g sugar

Smoothie with Strawberry Shortcake

One Servings

Ingredients

- 1/2 cup strawberry juice (120 mL)
- 1 tablespoon (60 g) strawberry yogurt
- 1/4 cup vanilla pudding mix (60 g)
- 1 teaspoon whipped cream
- 1 tablespoon crushed graham crackers
- As needed, ice cubes

Method

- Blend together the strawberry juice, yogurt, pudding mix, whipped cream, and graham cracker crumbs in a blender. Blend until the mixture is smooth and creamy.
- Blend in the ice cubes until the smoothie achieves the desired consistency.
- Serve the smoothie in a big glass or dish.

Nutritional Information

- 260 calories
- 7 g protein
- Fat: 7 g
- 44 g carbohydrate
- 1 g fiber
- 36 g sugar

Smoothie with Banana Split

One Servings

Ingredients

- 1/2 cup (120 mL) milk (or other non-dairy milk of choice)
- 1/4 cup (60 g) peeled and sliced banana
- 1/4 cup vanilla yogurt (60 g)
- 1 teaspoon chocolate syrup
- 1 teaspoon whipped cream
- 1 tablespoon nuts, chopped
- As needed, ice cubes

Method

- Blend together the milk, banana, yogurt, and chocolate syrup in a blender. Blend until smooth and creamy.

- Blend in the ice cubes until the smoothie achieves the desired consistency.
- Garnish with whipped cream and chopped nuts and serve.

Nutritional Information

- 320 calories
- 9 g protein
- Fat: 14 g
- 46 g carbohydrate
- 3 g fiber
- 36 g sugar

Smoothie with Chocolate Peanut Butter Cups

One Servings

Ingredients

- 1/2 cup (120 mL) chocolate milk (or your favorite non-dairy chocolate milk)
- 1 tablespoon (60 g) chocolate yogurt
- 1/4 cup (60 g) of creamy peanut butter
- 1 teaspoon tiny chocolate chips
- As needed, ice cubes

Method

- In a blender, combine the chocolate milk, yogurt, peanut butter, and chocolate chips. Blend until smooth and nutty.
- Blend in the ice cubes until the smoothie achieves the desired consistency.
- Serve the smoothie in a big glass or dish.

Nutritional Information

- Calories: 480
- Protein: 19 g
- Fat: 31 g
- 42 g carbohydrate
- Fiber: 4 g
- 34 g sugar

Black Forest Smoothie

One Servings

Ingredients

- 1/2 cup (120 ml) of cherry juice
- 1 tablespoon (60 g) chocolate yogurt
- 1/4 cup (37 g) of canned or fresh cherries, pitted and diced
- 1 teaspoon chocolate syrup

- 1 teaspoon whipped cream
- As needed, ice cubes

Method

- In a blender, combine the cherry juice, yogurt, cherries, and chocolate syrup. Blend until smooth and decadent.
- Blend in the ice cubes until the smoothie achieves the desired consistency.
- Top with whipped cream and enjoy.

Nutritional Information

- 260 calories
- Protein: 6 g
- Fat: 5 g
- 50 g carbohydrates
- 2 g fiber
- 44 g sugar

Tiramisu Smoothie

One Servings

Ingredients

- 1/2 cup (120 ml) of brewed decaffeinated coffee, chilled
- 1 tablespoon (60 g) low-fat cream cheese
- 1/4 cup vanilla yogurt (60 g)
- 1 tablespoon of cocoa powder
- 1 tablespoon crushed graham crackers
- As needed, ice cubes

Method

- In a blender, combine the coffee, cream cheese, yogurt, cocoa powder, and graham cracker crumbs. Blend until smooth and rich.
- Blend in the ice cubes until the smoothie achieves the desired consistency.
- Serve the smoothie in a big glass or dish.

Nutritional Information

- 240 calories
- Protein: 11 g
- Fat: 10 g
- Carbohydrates: 28 g

- 3 g fiber
- Sugar: 18 g

CONCLUSION

People with gastroparesis may find that smoothies are a useful complement to their diet. In addition to giving relief from some of the symptoms connected with this illness, they provide an easy and nourishing method to absorb critical nutrients.

Smoothies provide a flexible alternative for controlling gastroparesis since they may be tailored to fit specific dietary demands and constraints.

Patients with gastroparesis may make smoothies that are soothing on the stomach, simple to digest, and rich in essential nutrients by choosing their components carefully.

Smoothies may be made to accommodate various nutritional needs, such as including low-fiber alternatives, tolerating allergies or intolerances, or to follow certain dietary regimens.

Easier vitamin absorption, more hydration, and easier digestion are all advantages of smoothies for those with gastroparesis. Smoothies are a filling and fulfilling alternative that is easy on the stomach and may be had as a snack, meal replacement, or supplement.

To choose the ingredients and portion proportions that are best for a person's requirements, it is crucial to speak with a nutritionist or healthcare professional.

Based on the severity of gastroparesis symptoms, specific dietary limitations, and general health state, they may provide tailored advice.

People with gastroparesis may take advantage of a diversity of tastes, textures, and minerals while controlling their symptoms and promoting overall wellness by including smoothies in their diet.

Smoothies make it simple and pleasurable to maintain a balanced diet by guaranteeing that vital nutrients are available even while experiencing digestive difficulties.

The smoothie recipes in this book should only be used as a starting point; it is essential to consult with medical specialists to customize them to your unique requirements.

Smoothies may be an effective tool for controlling gastroparesis and fostering optimum health with the right advice and experimentation. Salutations on your path to hydration, vigor, and enhanced health!

Made in the USA
Columbia, SC
22 October 2024

44908158R00046